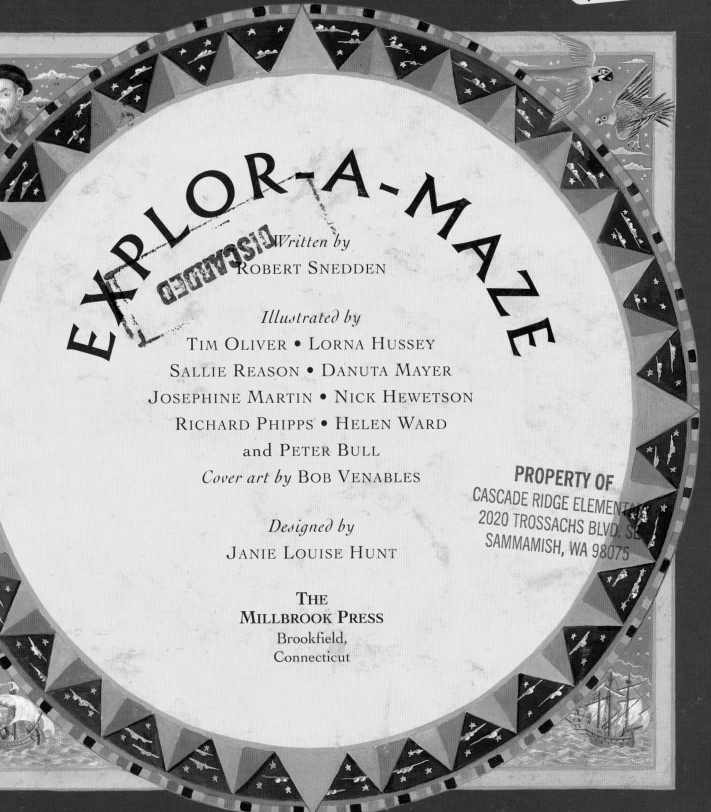

EXPLOR-A-MAZE

Written by
ROBERT SNEDDEN

Illustrated by
TIM OLIVER • LORNA HUSSEY
SALLIE REASON • DANUTA MAYER
JOSEPHINE MARTIN • NICK HEWETSON
RICHARD PHIPPS • HELEN WARD
and PETER BULL
Cover art by BOB VENABLES

Designed by
JANIE LOUISE HUNT

THE
MILLBROOK PRESS
Brookfield,
Connecticut

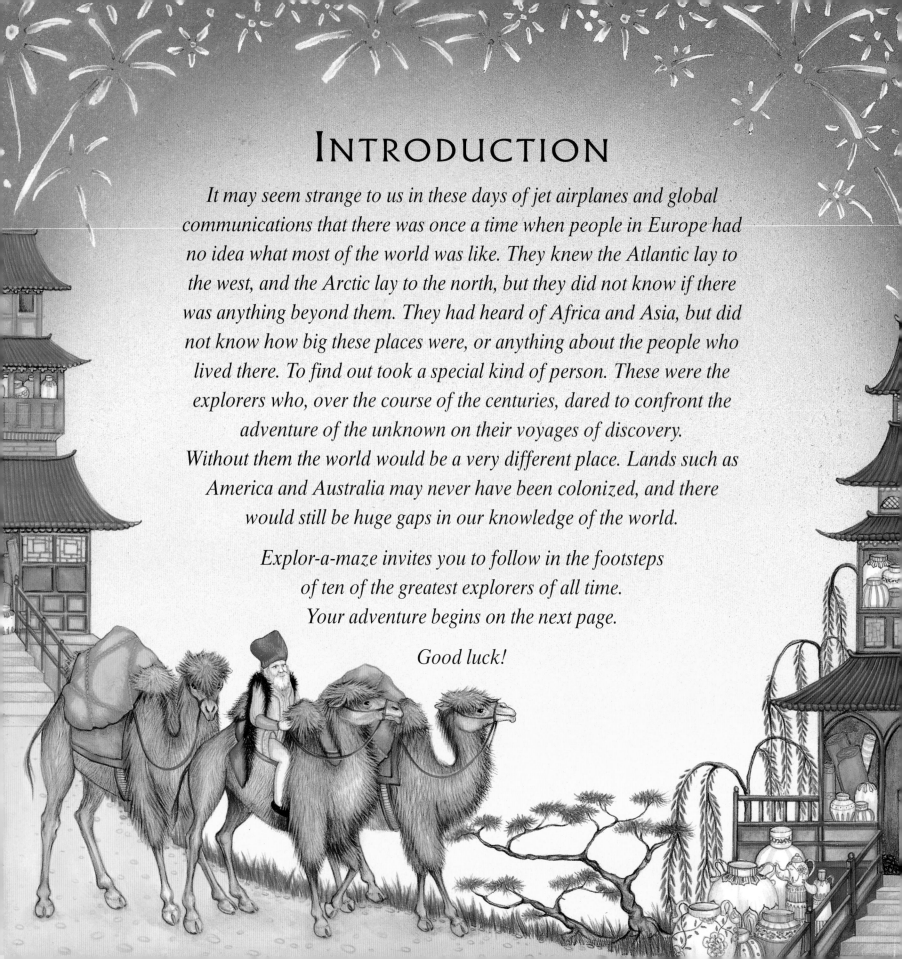

INTRODUCTION

It may seem strange to us in these days of jet airplanes and global communications that there was once a time when people in Europe had no idea what most of the world was like. They knew the Atlantic lay to the west, and the Arctic lay to the north, but they did not know if there was anything beyond them. They had heard of Africa and Asia, but did not know how big these places were, or anything about the people who lived there. To find out took a special kind of person. These were the explorers who, over the course of the centuries, dared to confront the adventure of the unknown on their voyages of discovery.
Without them the world would be a very different place. Lands such as America and Australia may never have been colonized, and there would still be huge gaps in our knowledge of the world.

Explor-a-maze invites you to follow in the footsteps of ten of the greatest explorers of all time. Your adventure begins on the next page.

Good luck!

THE EXPLORERS

LEIF ERIKSSON

1000

THE VIKINGS DISCOVER AMERICA

*Around A.D. 1000, Leif Eriksson became the first European
to land in America. He decided to spend the winter there, and every day
half of his band went off to explore while the others stayed behind.
One day his German friend Tyrkir disappeared. Leif had known Tyrkir since
he was a child and was very upset. He set out to look for him but soon saw
Tyrkir coming toward him looking very pleased. He had found what
seemed to be vines and grapes, so Leif called the new place Vinland.*

*To complete the maze opposite, you must help Leif to find Tyrkir,
but you must beware of wolves, bears, and pumas, which you cannot pass.
The Vikings did not have very good relations with the American peoples
they met, and so you must also avoid the crossed arrows.*

In the year A.D. 982, or thereabouts, Erik the Red, a tough adventurer who had been banished from his home in Norway for killing someone, was also thrown out of his new home, Iceland. Having nowhere else to go, he raised a crew and sailed west in search of new lands.

ERIK HAD NO CHARTS to guide him. All he knew was that a man called Gunnbjörn had seen a new coast when his ship was blown off course 50 years earlier.

1. After traveling for 450 miles (725 km) across the icy ocean, Erik and his crew reached land. The first thing they saw was a mighty glacier, but following the coast south, they found a land rich in grasslands and animals. Erik called the country Greenland.

2. Returning to Iceland in 985, Erik enlisted settlers for the new land. Of 25 ships that sailed for Greenland, just 14 arrived. One of those who set out was Bjarni Herjolfsson. Lost in a fog, Bjarni drifted off-course until he reached a new coast. He didn't land, but turned around and sailed back to join up with Erik.

3. Some 15 years later, Leif, who was Erik's son, bought Bjarni's boat. His plan was to find the new land for himself. With a crew of 35 Vikings Leif set out across the sea.

4. The first coast he saw had a striking landscape with flat slabs of stone projecting into the sea. Leif called this Helluland, or the "land of stone slabs." Many historians believe this must have been the southern part of Baffin Island, in northern Canada.

Map: GREENLAND, BAFFIN ISLAND, ICELAND, LABRADOR (North America), NEWFOUNDLAND, EUROPE, Atlantic Ocean

5. Leif and his crew now sailed south until they arrived at a coast with a lot of trees and white, sandy beaches. This was probably somewhere in the south of Labrador, in Canada. Erik called this Markland, or the "land of woods."

6. The Vikings continued on their journey, eventually reaching a land with a mild climate that was rich in natural resources. This was Vinland, or the "land of vines," and could have been near the northern tip of Newfoundland. It is unlikely that grapes grew there then, so some think Leif had really found huckleberries.

7. Leif Eriksson made no more voyages after he returned to Greenland. However, his brother Thorvald now bought his boat and set off to find the place Leif had described. He became the first westerner to encounter some of the people of the New World. It was not a happy meeting. The Vikings killed the first men they met, and Thorvald himself was killed by an arrow when the natives retaliated. It is not certain where this incident took place. It may have been in Labrador or farther south, near Nova Scotia or New Brunswick.

8. Thorvald's crew returned to Greenland with tales of the the Native Americans they had met. Other expeditions soon followed, and around 1020 a settlement was founded near the modern village of L'Anse-aux-Meadows, which is on the northern tip of

Newfoundland. Here a baby boy, Snorri, was born, the first European to be born in North America. The Vikings withdrew after three years, following a fight with the Americans. No more attempts were made to settle Vinland, and this story was thought to be a legend until remains of a Viking settlement were found in Canada in the 1960s.

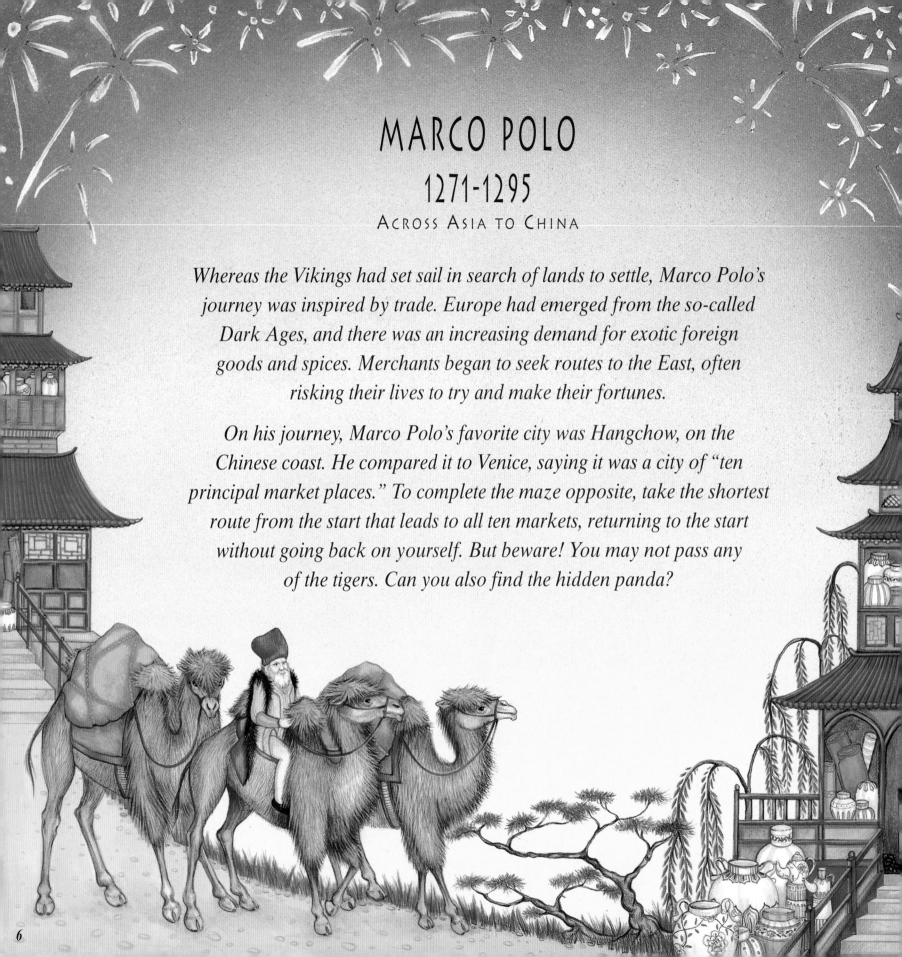

MARCO POLO

1271-1295

ACROSS ASIA TO CHINA

Whereas the Vikings had set sail in search of lands to settle, Marco Polo's journey was inspired by trade. Europe had emerged from the so-called Dark Ages, and there was an increasing demand for exotic foreign goods and spices. Merchants began to seek routes to the East, often risking their lives to try and make their fortunes.

On his journey, Marco Polo's favorite city was Hangchow, on the Chinese coast. He compared it to Venice, saying it was a city of "ten principal market places." To complete the maze opposite, take the shortest route from the start that leads to all ten markets, returning to the start without going back on yourself. But beware! You may not pass any of the tigers. Can you also find the hidden panda?

START

In the last half of the thirteenth century the city state of Venice enjoyed great power, and its merchants traveled far and wide in search of trading opportunities. To the east, Kublai Khan, the great Mongol leader, ruled over a vast empire that stretched over nearly the whole of central Asia.

IN VENICE were two merchant brothers, Niccolò and Maffeo Polo, who decided the time was right to open up trade links with the lands to the east.

1. While they were staying at Bukhara, a city in present-day Uzbekistan, the Polos met an envoy of Kublai Khan's, the Mongol emperor. The envoy described the riches of the Khan's court and told them that the Khan, who had never seen Europeans like them before, would be eager to meet them.

The Polos took a year to travel to the Khan's court at Cambaluc (now Beijing, the capital of China), becoming the first Europeans to cross Asia. The Khan treated them courteously, granting them safe conduct through his lands. Finally, in 1269, they arrived back at the Mediterranean, at Acre, and returned to Venice.

2. At the end of 1271 the Polos decided to return to Kublai Khan's court, and this time they took Niccolò's seventeen-year-old son Marco with them. They traveled through Turkey and Armenia, and then south through what is now Iran, until they reached the Persian Gulf. They had planned to sail to India, but thought the local ships too flimsy for the voyage.

3. Instead, the Polos traveled north again, then east, crossing the Pamir mountain range into China in the spring of 1272. Next, they had to cross the Takla Makan desert before reaching the rich, fertile lands of Khotan. Bad weather caused many delays, and it was more than three years before they got to

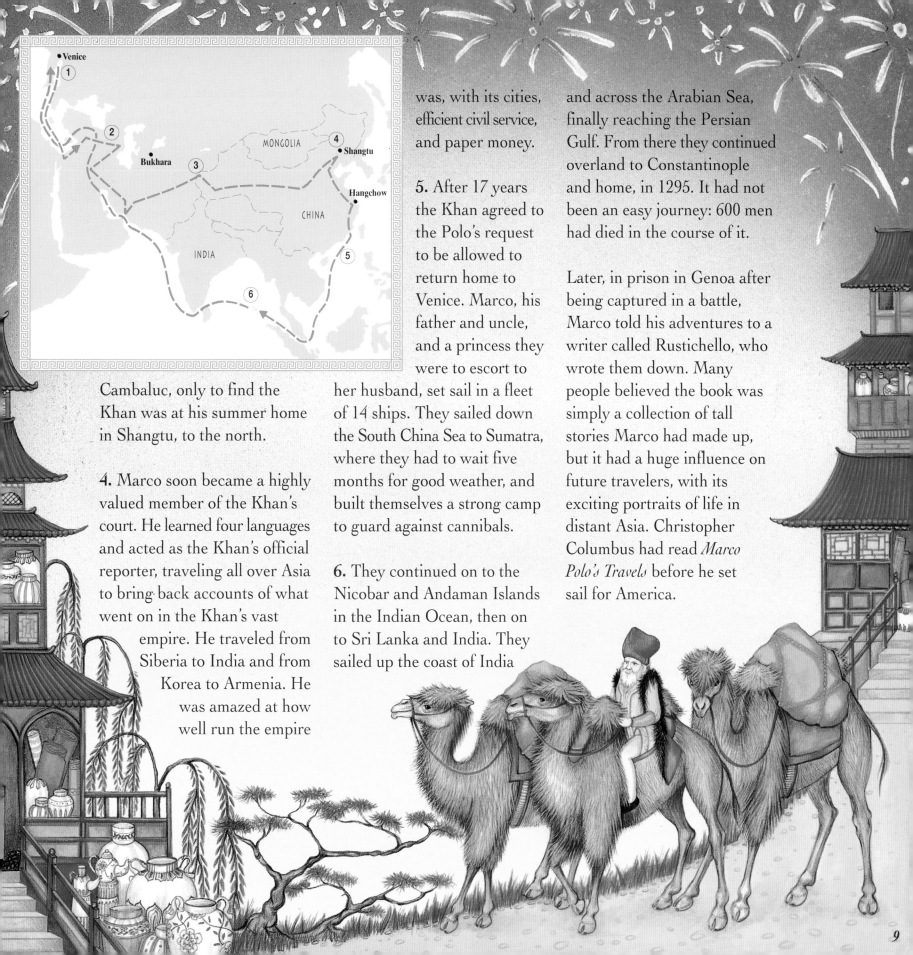

was, with its cities, efficient civil service, and paper money.

5. After 17 years the Khan agreed to the Polo's request to be allowed to return home to Venice. Marco, his father and uncle, and a princess they were to escort to her husband, set sail in a fleet of 14 ships. They sailed down the South China Sea to Sumatra, where they had to wait five months for good weather, and built themselves a strong camp to guard against cannibals.

6. They continued on to the Nicobar and Andaman Islands in the Indian Ocean, then on to Sri Lanka and India. They sailed up the coast of India and across the Arabian Sea, finally reaching the Persian Gulf. From there they continued overland to Constantinople and home, in 1295. It had not been an easy journey: 600 men had died in the course of it.

Later, in prison in Genoa after being captured in a battle, Marco told his adventures to a writer called Rustichello, who wrote them down. Many people believed the book was simply a collection of tall stories Marco had made up, but it had a huge influence on future travelers, with its exciting portraits of life in distant Asia. Christopher Columbus had read *Marco Polo's Travels* before he set sail for America.

Cambaluc, only to find the Khan was at his summer home in Shangtu, to the north.

4. Marco soon became a highly valued member of the Khan's court. He learned four languages and acted as the Khan's official reporter, traveling all over Asia to bring back accounts of what went on in the Khan's vast empire. He traveled from Siberia to India and from Korea to Armenia. He was amazed at how well run the empire

CHRISTOPHER COLUMBUS
1492
AMERICA REDISCOVERED

*When Christopher Columbus set sail across the uncharted Atlantic Ocean in 1492,
the story of Leif Eriksson's intrepid voyage to Vinland was almost forgotten.
Still, many educated people had read about Marco Polo's adventures in the East, and
Columbus hoped he might find a profitable sea route to India and China by sailing
west. Little did he know that the continent of America lay directly in his path.*

*Columbus and his crew saw many new things on their voyage.
To complete the maze, start at San Salvador, finish at the Santa María,
and collect the following in any order: 1 pumpkin, 2 tropical fish, 3 pineapples,
2 parrots, and 2 corn cobs. You must not double back, and
you must avoid whirlpools, storms, natives in canoes,
coral reefs, whales, and islands with cannibals.*

tropical fish

parrots

whirlpool

pumpkin

cannibals

angry natives

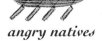

pineapple

corn cob

coral reefs

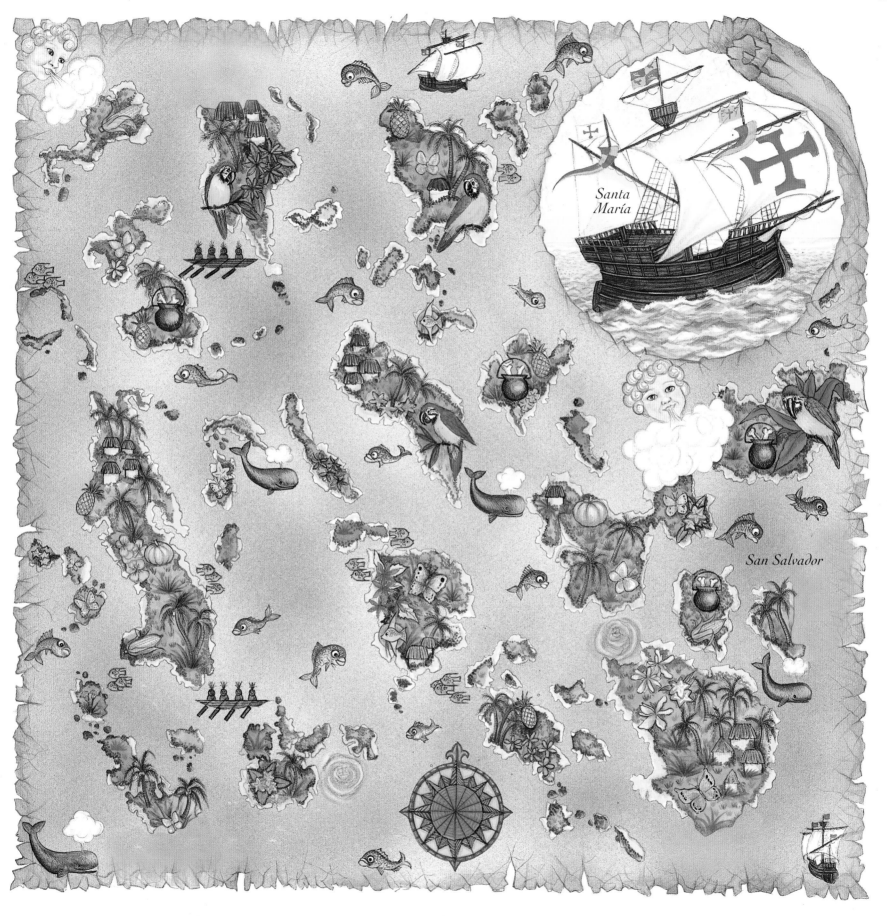

Santa María

San Salvador

Toward the end of the 1400s, the Portuguese were trying to find an eastern sea route to the fabulous places Marco Polo had written about. Christopher Columbus, a sailor from Genoa, believed a way could be found by sailing west. He longed to reach China or Japan and bring back gold, silk, and spices.

COLUMBUS went to see the King of Portugal, who refused to help him, and so he traveled to Spain. At first the Spanish wouldn't help him either — they were at war. But after defeating their enemies, the king and queen of Spain met Columbus and agreed to his plan.

1. Columbus had three ships made ready. They were the *Santa María*, the *Niña*, and the *Pinta*, and they set sail on August 3, 1492, stopping in the Canaries before setting out again. Columbus thought a trip to China wouldn't take very long, but soon the ships had been at sea for a month.

2. The easterly winds had helped Columbus to travel quickly, but the crew became afraid there would be no westerly winds to take them back home. After thirty days at sea, Columbus agreed that if land wasn't sighted within three days, they would turn back.

3. Two days later, on October 12, 1492, the lookout man on the *Pinta* sighted land, and soon Columbus had set foot on an island. He named it San Salvador, and it seemed a wonderful place — food was plentiful and the people were helpful and kind. But things weren't peaceful for long. The sailors took the natives' gold, captured some of them, and loaded up their ships with goods.

4. Columbus spent two weeks discovering and naming more islands. He found Santa María de la Concepción, Ferdinanda, Juana, and Hispaniola (now the Dominican Republic and Haiti). Unfortunately, the *Santa María* was damaged and had to be abandoned. Columbus left some men in Hispaniola and set sail for Spain. When he arrived he was given a hero's welcome. He was put in charge of a new expedition, and seventeen ships set sail on September 25, 1493.

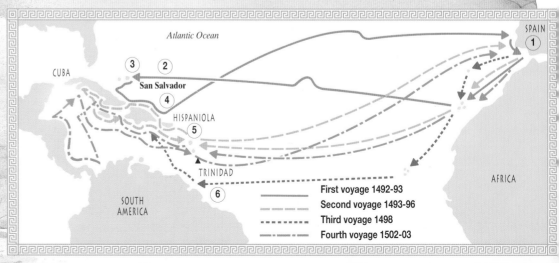

First voyage 1492-93
Second voyage 1493-96
Third voyage 1498
Fourth voyage 1502-03

5. On his second voyage Columbus set out to return to Hispaniola, but on the way he found a number of new islands, among them Dominica, Guadalupe, and Puerto Rico. Returning to Hispaniola, Columbus found to his horror that all the men there had been killed. As a result, he set up a fort inland and also a town called Isabela, which he intended to govern. Unfortunately, Columbus proved to be a bad governor and after a couple of years he had to return to Spain to explain himself. There he was given the command of a third expedition, which set out in May 1498.

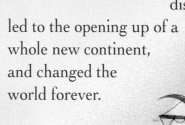

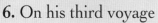

6. On his third voyage Columbus headed south, finding Trinidad, near Venezuela. He noticed that the sea there was not so salty, and guessed there must be a large river nearby. This was true—he was close to the mouth of the mighty Orinoco.

Columbus returned to Hispaniola, where things were going from bad to worse. The King and Queen sent out an investigator, and this time Columbus was sent back to Spain in chains. Still, they soon forgave him and allowed him to command a fourth expedition, although he was forbidden to ever return to Hispaniola.

His fourth expedition under way, Columbus headed for Santo Domingo, passing Martinique on the way. There the new governor refused to let him land, and so Columbus continued his voyage, eventually landing on the Islas de la Bahia, near Honduras. He followed the coast south, passing Nicaragua, Costa Rica, and Panama before returning to Spain for the last time in 1504. Columbus would never captain an expedition again and, in the end, the man who had discovered America died poor and forgotten in the Spanish city of Valladolid in the year 1506. But his discoveries led to the opening up of a whole new continent, and changed the world forever.

VASCO DA GAMA
1497
THE SEA ROUTE TO INDIA

*While Columbus was busy with his explorations to the west,
the Portuguese had been trying to find a route around
Africa to trade with the rich lands of India and China.
In 1497, King Manuel of Portugal sent an expedition,
led by Vasco da Gama, to travel around the southern tip
of Africa to discover whether or not they could reach India.*

*On the final leg of his voyage, da Gama sailed from
Malindi, on Africa's east coast, finding his way
across the Indian Ocean to Calicut, in India.
To complete the maze opposite,
you must help him by finding the route to
Calicut—not Goa!—that passes three friendly
boats, or dhows, with yellow sails.*

Arabia

India

Goa

Calicut

Africa

Malindi

N

Indian
Ocean

15

In 1487, King John of Portugal had sent an expedition, led by Bartolomeu Dias, to the southern tip of Africa. The king named the place that Dias reached "the Cape of Good Hope," because it seemed to offer the possibility of a sea route to India.

UNFORTUNATELY, war and the death of King John delayed the sending of an expedition around the Cape to India for almost 10 years.

1. Finally, in 1495, King Manuel appointed Vasco da Gama, a man with little experience, to explore the sea route around Africa. Four ships set out from Lisbon on July 8, 1497.

2. In the early part of the voyage da Gama's flagship was separated from the others for 10 days before they all met up in the Cape Verde islands in the Atlantic. For 3 months the ships sailed out of sight of land down the middle of the Atlantic.

3. They eventually put in to a bay just north of the Cape of Good Hope, which they named Santa Helena. While they were making repairs there, an unfortunate misunderstanding with the natives resulted in da Gama being slightly wounded.

4. On November 22 the ships rounded the Cape. After anchoring for a while in what is now called Mossel Bay, and having more trouble with the locals, the expedition sailed on around the southeast coast of Africa, becoming the first Europeans to do so.

5. They came across people who were very friendly toward them and helped them find fresh water. These were the Bantu, whom the Portuguese called Boa Gente, or good people. The Portuguese discovered a new river here, the Limpopo, which they named Rio Cobre.

6. Reaching Mozambique, da Gama found evidence that the people were trading with India. But once again he also found a hostile welcome. He didn't improve matters by firing his cannon at some armed men on the shore.

7. The King of Mombasa promised the voyagers a friendly welcome if they came ashore. However, da Gama discovered that the king had been plotting to capture them and punish them for their actions in Mozambique.

8. The Portuguese sailed on to Malindi, finding a warmer welcome there. Da Gama asked the local sultan to find him someone who could guide the ships to India. A navigator was found, and on April 24, 1498 the expedition set sail across the Indian Ocean. Within a month they had reached Calicut on the southwest coast of India.

9. Da Gama was introduced to the Zamorin, the local ruler. Things went well at first, but da Gama soon found himself in difficulties again. The Zamorin thought the "gifts" da Gama had brought from Portugal were cheap and insulting, and both sides grew impatient with each other. Eventually the Zamorin offered to trade his spices and precious stones for gold and silver. This seemed to be the best deal the Portuguese would get, and they headed for home.

10. They were dogged by bad weather, and it took them more than three months to cross the Arabian Sea to Africa, reaching Mogadishu on January 2, 1499. They carried on to Malindi, where they restocked with fresh supplies, then headed for home. Vasco da Gama sailed back into Lisbon in September 1499.

Many men had died on the journey, including da Gama's own brother, but his voyage opened the way for many other expeditions. The first one to leave, under the command of Pedro Cabral, actually sailed so far to the west of the African coast that they discovered Brazil!

PORTUGAL

AFRICA

INDIA

• Calicut

Malindi •

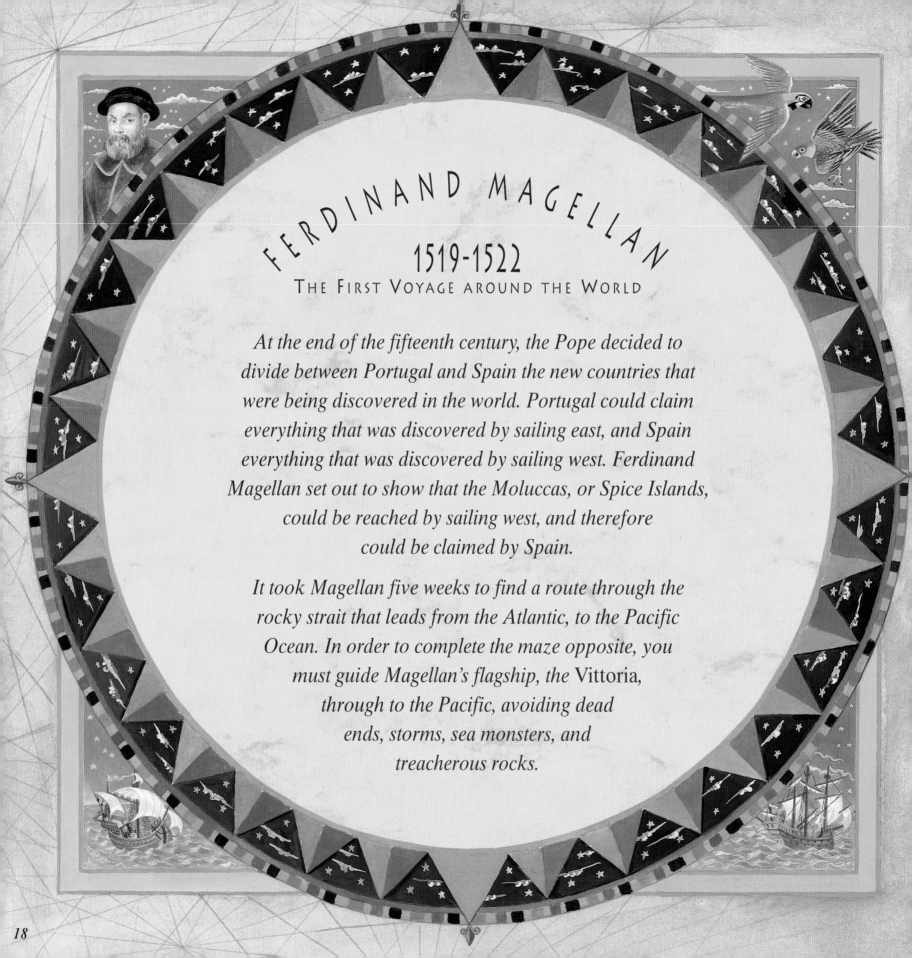

FERDINAND MAGELLAN

1519-1522

THE FIRST VOYAGE AROUND THE WORLD

At the end of the fifteenth century, the Pope decided to divide between Portugal and Spain the new countries that were being discovered in the world. Portugal could claim everything that was discovered by sailing east, and Spain everything that was discovered by sailing west. Ferdinand Magellan set out to show that the Moluccas, or Spice Islands, could be reached by sailing west, and therefore could be claimed by Spain.

It took Magellan five weeks to find a route through the rocky strait that leads from the Atlantic, to the Pacific Ocean. In order to complete the maze opposite, you must guide Magellan's flagship, the Vittoria, through to the Pacific, avoiding dead ends, storms, sea monsters, and treacherous rocks.

N

M

3

S

Pacific
Ocean

Vittoria

*Ferdinand Magellan
was born in Portugal around the year 1480.
After serving with the Portuguese in the East Indies and
in Morocco, where he was lamed for life, he became unhappy
with his country when his achievements were not recognized.*

IN 1517, Magellan left for Spain, where he told the king, Charles V, that he would find him a sea route west to the Moluccas, or Spice Islands. Charles gave him five ships.

1. On September 20, 1519, Magellan sailed from the Guadalquivir River in Spain with the five ships and 265 men. They were clumsy ships with towering forecastles and round-bottomed, leaking hulls. The sailors had to work constantly with wooden pumps in order to keep them afloat. At best, the ships, which had only three sails each, could make three knots when a fair wind was blowing. The crews had no shelter at all and ate and slept on the decks in all kinds of weather, soaked by waves and rain and exposed to the sun and wind. Magellan had no charts and no way of working out his position accurately either. Under these adverse conditions he set sail for the unknown.

2. The little fleet made its way safely across the Atlantic, reaching Rio de Janeiro on December 13, where they restocked their supplies. From here they sailed south, mapping and exploring the coasts of Brazil and Argentina and searching for a route to the west. The farther south they traveled the worse the weather became. Antarctic storms began to lash the armada. Conditions grew so bad that three of the ships' captains staged a mutiny. Magellan, the seasoned campaigner, captured their three ships and kept command of the fleet.

3. The smallest ship was wrecked as Magellan searched for the passage to the Pacific. Then, on October 21, 1520, two ships sailing up an inlet found salt water rather than fresh: the "Straits of Magellan" had been found. Although supplies were running low and no one knew what lay on the other side, Magellan sailed onward.

4. Snow-capped mountains loomed high above the little ships, and strong tides tore through the rocky straits, as a fierce wind blew from the west and the sailors were forced to use rowing boats to tow the ships through. The largest ship deserted, turning back for Spain. Magellan, afraid it had disappeared, searched for it.

5. Finally, on November 28, the three remaining ships emerged from the strait out into the open waters. Magellan turned to his officers and said, "Gentlemen, these are waters no ship has sailed in before." Setting a northwesterly course, they headed across the new ocean. Magellan thought they would reach the Spice Islands in about a month. He was wrong.

6. The three ships sailed across the ocean out of sight of land for a hundred days, and many of the sailors fell ill. Finally, on March 6, 1521, they reached the island of Guam, where they resupplied and set out for the Philippines.

7. Here, on April 27, Magellan was killed when he became involved in a local dispute. The tiny fleet continued sailing west, but only one ship, the *Vittoria*, with just 18 men aboard, finally made it back to Spain in September 1522. These few men had completed the first voyage around the world.

ASIA

EUROPE

NORTH AMERICA

Pacific Ocean

Atlantic Ocean

7 GUAM

AFRICA

PHILIPPINES

6

SOUTH AMERICA

5

2

3

4 *Straits of Magellan*

1

CAPTAIN JAMES COOK

1768-1771

SEARCH FOR THE SOUTHERN CONTINENT

*In the course of three epic voyages of discovery spanning more
than ten years, Captain James Cook helped to fill in the gaps
in the maps of the Pacific and Southern Oceans.*

*One of Cook's companions on the first voyage was Sir Joseph Banks,
the great naturalist. As they explored the coast of Australia, they
saw many new plants and animals and caught sight of the
native people of Australia, the Aboriginals, watching them.*

To complete the maze you must leave Cook's ship, the Endeavour,
*and collect 10 new plant specimens without doubling back
(although you may cross your path if necessary).
To finish, you must return to the* Endeavour *again.*

In the middle of the eighteenth century there were still many gaps to be filled in the map of the Pacific Ocean. One man, Captain James Cook, did more to fill in the blanks than any other.

WHEN COOK took command of an expedition to the Pacific to make astronomical observations, he was already a first-class seaman with over 20 years of experience behind him. His ship, the *Endeavour*, had a crew of 93, besides himself, and included a team of 11 scientists.

1. At the end of August 1768, Cook and his men headed for George III Island, which is known today as Tahiti. Intrigue surrounded the expedition, because Cook had been given sealed instructions before he left. After their scientific mission had been accomplished, in June 1769, Cook opened the instructions. He was to sail south from Tahiti to search for Terra Australis Incognita—the "Unknown Southern Land," which it was believed must exist somewhere in the vast Pacific.

2. More than a hundred years earlier, in 1642, the Dutch sailor Abel Tasman had discovered the land now called New Zealand. Finding nothing south of Tahiti, Cook now sailed west to New Zealand. For the next six months Cook sailed right around both the North and South Islands of New Zealand, compiling a highly detailed map of the coastline.

3. On April 1, 1770, the *Endeavour* headed west again in search of the coast of New Holland, now called Australia, first landed on by Europeans in 1605. On April 28, Cook dropped anchor in a bay that had such a huge number of unknown plants growing around it that he named it Botany Bay.

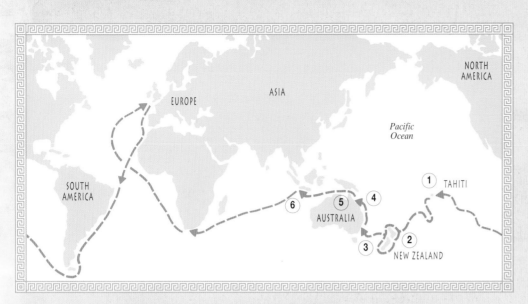

for extensive repairs. Cook then sailed for home, via Capetown, arriving in England on July 13, 1771. He had sailed all the way around the world.

Cook undertook two more Pacific voyages. On his second voyage, in the *Resolution*, he sailed south until pack ice turned him back, finally deciding there was no "southern continent."

His third voyage took him north. On the way he discovered the Hawaiian Islands. He sailed as far north as he could up the west coast of North America until, again, ice blocked the way. There was, it seemed, no northern passage from the Pacific to the Atlantic. Cook returned to Hawaii where, on February 14, 1779, a misunderstanding led to his death at the hands of some Hawaiians.

4. Sailing north, the expedition almost met with disaster when the *Endeavour* was holed by the Great Barrier Reef that lies off Australia's northeast coast. It took an immense effort by the crew to refloat the *Endeavour* and nurse her into harbor.

5. Cook and his men spent two months near present-day Cooktown trying to patch up their damaged ship as best they could. By August 21 they had sailed the still-leaking *Endeavour* to the northernmost tip of Australia, Cape York, and once again Cook set a course for the west.

6. At the beginning of October, the *Endeavour* sailed into Batavia (now Jakarta) in Indonesia

LEWIS AND CLARK
1804-1806
ACROSS THE ROCKY MOUNTAINS TO THE PACIFIC

*In May 1804, Meriwether Lewis and William Clark,
soldiers in the United States Army, led an expedition to the Pacific
Ocean west across thousands of miles of largely unknown lands.
Both men kept journals, and theirs was a story of adventure and often hardship.
There was help along the way, too, from many of the Indian nations they
encountered on their journey, such as the Mandan, Shoshone, and Nez Percé.*

*Here the expedition is searching for a route across a high
mountain pass. Rockfalls, and the occasional
grizzly bear, block some of the more obvious routes.
Can you help them find the way and set them
on the trail to the Shoshone village?*

START

FINISH

In the eighteenth century, explorers, adventurers, traders, and trappers gradually began to open up the vast areas of North America that lay beyond the Great Lakes and the Appalachian Mountains. The Rocky Mountains appeared like a great barrier blocking the route to the Pacific. No one knew how far the range stretched, and people hoped that a quick way around the mountains might be discovered.

AS SO OFTEN HAPPENED, the spur that drove the explorers was the hope of finding shorter trade routes to the Far East. In 1793, Alexander Mackenzie had crossed from one side of Canada to the other, and so, naturally, the American government felt that they too should find a way overland to the Pacific.

In 1803, President Thomas Jefferson persuaded Congress to allocate funds for an expedition and appointed Captain Meriwether Lewis to lead it. Lewis and Lieutenant William Clark, his second in command, were experienced soldiers and resourceful outdoorsmen. Clark had a particular gift for finding his way across unknown territory.

1. That winter Lewis and Clark assembled 40-odd men to form their "Corps of Discovery," and, in May 1804, they set off up the Missouri from St Louis. They had three boats and a number of horses, which followed the boats along the riverbank. As they moved slowly northwest, past the site of present-day Sioux City, Iowa, they saw vast herds of buffalo on the prairies and also encountered prairie dogs.

2. By October they had reached the villages of the Mandan people in North Dakota. They received a warm welcome and settled down to wait out a harsh winter before traveling on. They learned a great deal from the Mandan about the country that lay ahead, and a young Shoshone woman, Sacajawea, agreed to act as guide for the expedition.

3. In spring, the party set off again. Sacajawea brought her baby with her, carrying him on her back. Traveling west, they came to the spot where the Missouri was joined by the Yellowstone. Here they killed their first grizzly bear.

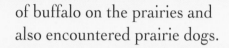

4. By June they had reached the Great Falls of the Missouri, in Montana. Getting past these 400-foot (120-meter) high waterfalls meant leaving the river to haul all the equipment and supplies across land on crude wheeled carts they made. This job took them three weeks.

5. Back on the river again, the next obstacle they came to was the Big Belt Mountains, the beginning of the mighty Rockies. They turned southward, arriving at the place where three streams join to form the Missouri. One of the forks would take them west again, and they decided to name it the Jefferson River.

6. Crossing the Rockies through the Lemhi Pass, Lewis and Clark's men were forced to abandon their boats and continue the journey on foot. They turned north in the shadow of the Bitteroot Mountains. Here they met a traveling group of Shoshone, one of whom turned out to be Sacajawea's brother.

7. At the end of August the explorers set out north again down the Bitteroot valley, before turning southwest at Lolo Pass to find that they had at last left the Rockies behind them.

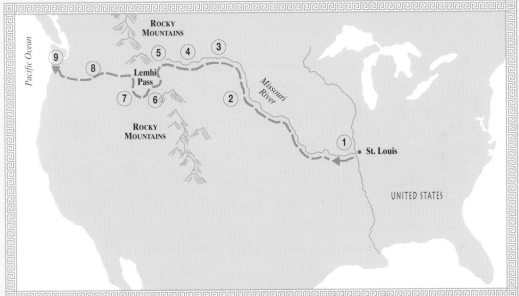

They came to the Clearwater River and again took to the water in dugout canoes, leaving their horses in the care of some Nez Percé they had met.

8. By the end of October that year, Lewis and Clark's expedition had followed the Clearwater and Snake Rivers until they reached the great Columbia River. The Columbia took them still farther

west, and they sped swiftly through the Cascade Mountain range, swept along by wild rapids.

9. Finally, on November 15, 1805, 18 months and 4,000 miles (6,430 km) after first setting out, the expedition reached the mouth of the Columbia on the shores of the Pacific Ocean, becoming the first Europeans to take that route. There was, as Clark recorded in his journal, "great joy in camp."

DAVID LIVINGSTONE
1841-1873
INTO THE HEART OF AFRICA

*Dr. David Livingstone was one of the greatest
of the European explorers who traveled in the vast continent
of Africa. He had originally gone there as a medical man
and a missionary, but he soon became committed to the idea
of discovery. He investigated huge areas of central Africa
and made many discoveries, including the Victoria Falls
and Lake Nyasa (now called Lake Malawi).*

*To complete the maze you must help the famous reporter
Stanley to track down Livingstone. Can you lead him through
the jungle thickets to find the shortest route to the village
of Ujiji, near the shore of Lake Tanganyika?
You may cross the rivers and go along all of the paths,
except where they are blocked by animals.*

START

Ujiji

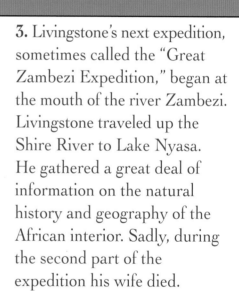

David Livingstone arrived in Africa in 1841 as a missionary, hoping to convert the Africans he met to Christianity. A deeply religious man, Livingstone had a great respect for the Africans and was a life-long opponent of the slave trade that brought suffering to so many of them.

IN 1841, he was stationed at Kuruman on the outskirts of the Kalahari Desert. Over the next few years he made several trips farther north looking for possible sites for new settlements. On one occasion he was mauled by a lion and was lucky to survive.

1. Livingstone's first real expedition came in 1849, when he set out from Kolobeng, in Botswana, in the company of his wife and children and a number of friends. The party crossed the Kalahari Desert to Lake Ngami; they were the first Europeans to see the lake. Livingstone was sure that a vast river system must lie to the north of the lake, and he wanted to explore it.

2. Between September 1854 and May 1856, Livingstone and his group traveled from central Africa to the west coast and then crossed the continent all the way back to the east coast, becoming the first Europeans to cross Africa from coast to coast. In November 1855 Livingstone came upon an incredible sight. The Africans called it the "Smoke that Thunders"—Livingstone named it the Victoria Falls after the British Queen Victoria.

3. Livingstone's next expedition, sometimes called the "Great Zambezi Expedition," began at the mouth of the river Zambezi. Livingstone traveled up the Shire River to Lake Nyasa. He gathered a great deal of information on the natural history and geography of the African interior. Sadly, during the second part of the expedition his wife died.

4. Livingstone's last African journey began in 1866, when he set out to investigate Lake Nyasa and the rivers of Central Africa. In particular he wanted to try to find the sources of the Nile River and the Congo.

Starting from Zanzibar, Livingstone sailed south along the coast and then up the Rovuma River with a company of 60 Africans.

5. Livingstone reached the shores of Lake Tanganyika in April 1867. He was quite ill at this time, a situation that was not helped by the theft of his medicine chest. After resting for a while he continued on, discovering Lake Mweru and and Lake Bangwelu. He grew increasingly ill, however, and returned to Lake Tanganyika in 1871. Meanwhile stories were reaching London that Livingstone was missing, perhaps dead. A reporter for the *New York Herald*, Henry M. Stanley, was sent out by the newspaper to find Livingstone. When Stanley finally reached the explorer, he greeted him with the now-famous words, "Dr. Livingstone, I presume?"

Stanley gave Livingstone medicine, and he grew strong enough to travel again, joining Stanley to explore the north of Lake Tanganyika and the lands to the east. At the end of the expedition, in 1872, Stanley tried to convince Livingstone to return to England, but he refused.

Livingstone traveled south again, determined to find the source of the Nile and to help end the slave trade. At last, in May 1873, Livingstone's long illness got the better of him, and he was found dead. His African companions buried his heart and internal organs in Africa, taking his body to London, where it is buried in Westminster Abbey.

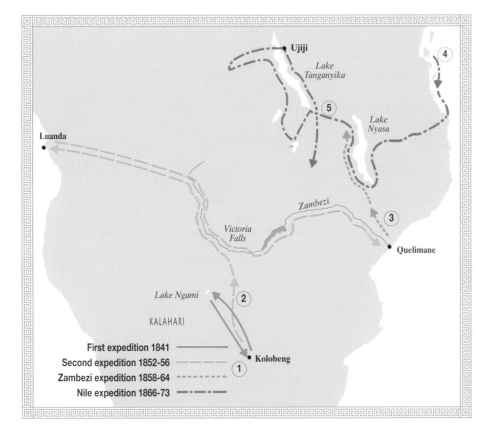

Luanda

Ujiji

Lake Tanganyika

Lake Nyasa

Zambezi

Victoria Falls

Quelimane

Lake Ngami

KALAHARI

Kolobeng

First expedition 1841
Second expedition 1852-56
Zambezi expedition 1858-64
Nile expedition 1866-73

ROALD AMUNDSEN

1910-1911

THE RACE TO THE SOUTH POLE

The Norwegian Roald Amundsen was one of the greatest of the polar explorers. One of his accomplishments was finally proving that a northwest passage between the Atlantic and the Pacific Oceans actually existed when he took his motorized sailing ship Gjöa through it in 1906. In the course of the voyage Amundsen learned a lot from the native Inuit about polar survival.

Probably the greatest of Amundsen's feats was being the first man to reach the South Pole. Amundsen used the experience he gained from his time spent with the Inuit in the Arctic to get himself and his team to the South Pole and back again safely. Robert Scott's famous expedition to the South Pole was, by contrast, badly planned and ended in tragic failure.

Here, Amundsen and his team are attempting to find a route up the Axel Helberg Glacier. To complete the maze you must work your way up to the top of the glacier by the shortest route, collecting three food parcels after you leave base camp. Note that the crevasses are impassable unless they are marked with a ladder or ice pick.

FINISH

START

35

*In 1909, Roald Amundsen had been preparing
for an ambitious expedition: to drift across the frozen
Arctic Ocean in his ship* Fram *and perhaps reach the North Pole.
However, news reached him in September that Robert Peary had
claimed to have made it to the Pole. Amundsen changed his plans
and decided to head for the South Pole instead.*

AMUNDSEN kept his plans secret. He knew that the Englishman Robert Scott was also planning an assault on the South Pole, and he did not wish to cause the Norwegian government embarrassment by openly mounting a rival expedition.

The *Fram* sailed from Norway on June 7, 1910. It was not until early September, when he reached Madeira, that Amundsen announced his intentions. With the full support of his crew, Amundsen made a dash for Antarctica.

1. In January 1911, the *Fram* reached the Ross Ice Shelf, and the crew built Framheim, a group of huts and tents where the polar party and their 100 dogs would spend the winter. The *Fram* and the rest of the crew left for a voyage in the Southern Ocean.

2. That winter, Amundsen and his team laid supply depots across the ice shelf on the route to the Pole. In late August, Amundsen made a try for the Pole, but was forced to turn back by the intense cold.

3. Finally, on October 15, Amundsen, with four men and 42 dogs, set out. The Pole lay 1,400 miles (2,250 km) away, and the toughest part of the journey took the five men and their superb dog teams 10,000 feet (3,000 meters) up the steep Axel Helberg Glacier to reach the polar plateau.

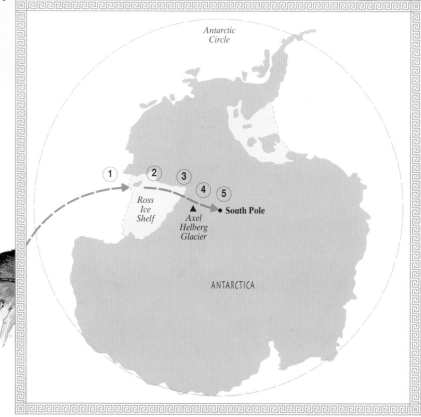

Antarctic Circle

Ross Ice Shelf

Axel Helberg Glacier

• **South Pole**

ANTARCTICA

4. Amundsen was no sentimentalist. At the top of the glacier all except 18 of the dogs were shot to provide food for the rest. On December 14 the party reached the South Pole. They took very careful measurements to make sure they were really there before planting the Norwegian flag. They pitched a tent at the Pole, which they called Polheim, or "Pole House."

5. The team left much of their equipment behind and, traveling light, managed to make the return journey to Framheim in just 41 days. They were expert skiers and made full use of their skills coming down the glaciers. When they reached their base they found the *Fram* waiting for them. The jubilant party set sail for Norway and home.

The journey to the Pole was not an easy one. Amundsen's team had to cope with unknown, icy terrain broken by treacherous crevasses and with the bitter cold. It was superb teamwork, training, and skill that saw them through safely. The contrast with Scott's expedition could not be more tragic. Scott took ponies, which experience and common sense should have told him were not suitable animals for the Antarctic. He also failed to set up proper supply depots for the journey. He and his men ended up hauling their heavy sleds themselves, an effort that probably fatally weakened them. Scott's team reached the Pole nearly five weeks after Amundsen. Their return journey, the men tired and demoralized at having been beaten by the Norwegians, was a nightmare. None of the five who reached the Pole survived. Scott's Antarctic expedition was one of the great failures of exploration.

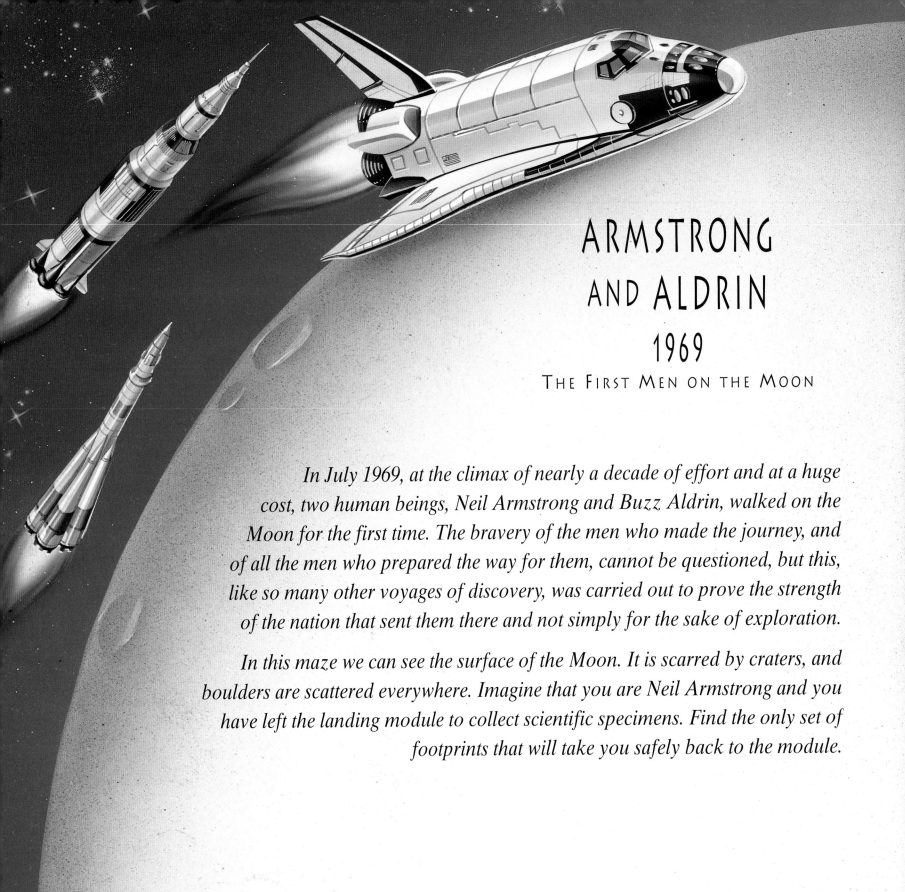

ARMSTRONG AND ALDRIN

1969

In July 1969, at the climax of nearly a decade of effort and at a huge cost, two human beings, Neil Armstrong and Buzz Aldrin, walked on the Moon for the first time. The bravery of the men who made the journey, and of all the men who prepared the way for them, cannot be questioned, but this, like so many other voyages of discovery, was carried out to prove the strength of the nation that sent them there and not simply for the sake of exploration.

In this maze we can see the surface of the Moon. It is scarred by craters, and boulders are scattered everywhere. Imagine that you are Neil Armstrong and you have left the landing module to collect scientific specimens. Find the only set of footprints that will take you safely back to the module.

A MASSIVE program began. Fleets of unmanned satellites and landers were sent to the Moon to map the surface and find suitable landing sites. Astronauts took off into Earth's orbit in the two-man Gemini capsule to learn the skills they would need for the Moon flight.

The Apollo program started in tragedy when three astronauts died in a capsule fire in January 1967. Four successful flights after that, including a dress rehearsal for the lunar landing that came within 15 miles (24 km) of the Moon's surface, set the scene for Apollo 11.

On April 12, 1961, the government of the USSR—the country that used to be centered on Russia—made an announcement that stunned and amazed people all over the world. That day, Colonel Yuri Gagarin, aboard the spacecraft Vostok, *had made one complete orbit of the Earth. This was the time of the Cold War, and there was bitter rivalry between the USSR and the US, the two most powerful nations on Earth. Each side wanted to outdo the other. The President of the the United States at the time was John F. Kennedy, and he wanted to find a way to meet the Soviet challenge in space. A month after Gagarin's flight he declared that the US would put a man on the moon within ten years.*

1. On July 16, 1969, Neil Armstrong, mission commander, Edwin "Buzz" Aldrin, lunar module pilot, and Michael Collins, command module pilot, were strapped into their capsule on top of a 305-foot (107-meter) Saturn V rocket. Huge crowds gathered to watch the launch as the mighty rocket engines lifted the astronauts into the sky on a column of flame.

2. One by one the rocket stages fell away as the craft continued to accelerate. Finally the third-stage rocket

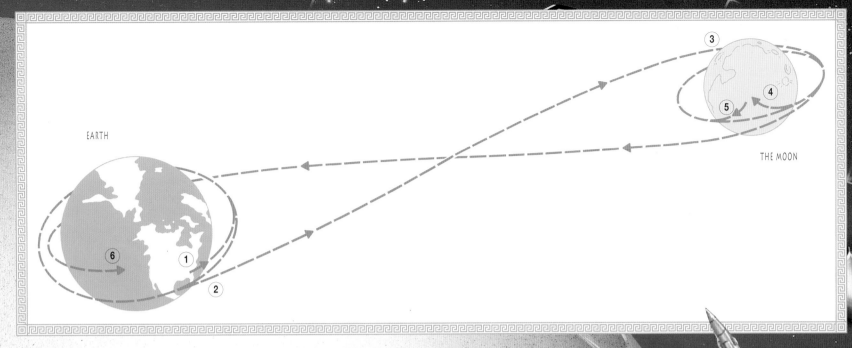

kicked in to boost the velocity to over 23,500 mph (38,000 km/h) and send them out of Earth's orbit and on their way to the Moon. Collins separated the command module, *Columbia*, from the third stage and moved it around to dock with the lunar module, *Eagle*, housed in the top of the third stage. The now-empty third-stage booster was sent on a collision course with the Moon, and the combined spacecraft continued on its way.

3. Three days after leaving the Earth, Apollo 11 went into orbit about 60 miles (100 km) above the surface of the Moon. On July 20, Armstrong and Aldrin were given the go-ahead from Mission Control at Houston to begin their descent to the lunar surface, and the lunar module *Eagle* separated from *Columbia*, leaving Collins alone in orbit.

4. There were anxious faces back on Earth as Armstrong steered the lunar module over the cratered and boulder-strewn surface to a safe landing in an area of the moon called the Sea of Tranquility. "Houston, Tranquility base here," he announced. "The *Eagle* has landed." Armstrong and Aldrin now began to prepare for the first moonwalk.

At 8:56 P.M. EDT, (1:56 GMT), Neil Armstrong climbed down the ladder of the lunar module and stepped onto the surface of the Moon. All over the world millions watched on television and heard the words, "That's one small step for a man. One giant leap for mankind." Fifteen minutes later Aldrin joined Armstrong, and for two hours they set up experiments and collected rock samples.

5. After 21 hours, the upper stage of the lunar module blasted them back into lunar orbit for a rendezvous with Collins. After Armstrong and Aldrin transferred back to the command module, the lunar module was crashed back onto the Moon. The service module engine was ignited to send the astronauts out of lunar orbit and back to Earth.

6. On July 24 the historic mission ended when the command module splashed down safely in the Pacific Ocean, and the crew was taken on board the aircraft carrier *USS Hornet*.

BIBLIOGRAPHY

If you are interested in reading more about the great explorers, you may find the following books useful:

Anderson, Dale. *Explorers Who Found New Worlds* (Twenty Events Series). Austin, TX: Raintree Steck-Vaughn, 1993.

Fritz, Jean. *Where Do You Think You're Going, Christopher Columbus?* NY: G.P. Putnam's Sons, 1980.

Haney, David. *Captain James Cook & the Explorers of the Pacific West* (World Explorers Series). Broomhall, PA: Chelsea House, 1992.

Langley, Andrew. *The Great Polar Adventure: The Journey of Roald Amundsen.* Broomhall, PA: Chelsea House, 1992.

Louri, Peter. *In the Path of Lewis and Clark: Traveling the Missouri.* Parsippany, NJ: Silver Burdett, 1996.

Lye, Keith. *Explorers* (The Silver Burdett Color Library). Parsippany, NJ: Silver Burdett, 1983.

Macdonald, Fiona. *Explorers: Expeditions and Pioneers* (Timeline Series). Danbury, CT: Franklin Watts, 1994.

Maestro, Betsy and Giulio Maestro. *The Discovery of the Americas.* NY: Lothrop, Lee & Shepard Books, 1991.

Mason, Anthony. *Peary and Amundsen Race to the Poles.* Austin, TX: Raintree Steck-Vaughn, 1995.

Mason, Anthony. *The Children's Atlas of Exploration.* Brookfield, CT: The Millbrook Press, 1993.

Maynard, Christopher. *Questions & Answers About Explorers.* NY: Kingfisher, 1995.

McGrath, Patrick. *The Lewis and Clark Expedition* (Turning Points in American History). NY: Silver Burdett, 1985.

Ryan, Peter. *Explorers & Mapmakers* (Time Detectives Series). NY: E.P. Dutton, 1990.

Saari, Peggy and Daniel B. Baker, eds. *Explorers & Discoverers: From Alexander the Great to Sally Ride.* Detroit: Gale, 1995.

Scheller, William. *The World's Greatest Explorers* (Profiles Series). Minneapolis: The Oliver Press, 1992.

Starkey, Dinah. *Scholastic Atlas of Exploration.* NY: Scholastic, 1993.

Stefoff, Rebecca. *Ferdinand Magellan & the Discovery of the World Ocean* (World Explorers Series). Broomhall, PA: Chelsea House, 1990.

Twist, Clint. *Magellan & da Gama* (Beyond the Horizons Series). Austin, TX: Raintree Steck-Vaughn, 1994.

—*Marco Polo: Overland to Medieval China* (Beyond the Horizons Series). Austin, TX: Raintree Steck-Vaughn, 1994.

—*Stanley & Livingstone: Expeditions Through Africa* (Beyond the Horizons Series). Austin, TX: Raintree Steck-Vaughn, 1995.